My Story in the Storm and Rain

Tiaina Doughty

My Story in the Storm and Rain

Copyright © 2022 Tiaina Doughty

ISBN: 979-8-218-05693-3

Publisher: Tiaina Doughty

Interior and cover design by
Williams DocuPrep
www.williamsdocuprep.com

<u>Dedication</u>

To my mom, Carol Doughty, everything I am you inspired me to be. To my dad, Carl Bowen, Sr. thank you for everything old man. To all my siblings, I love each of you. Special dedication to Carol's very own children: Felix Montiea Clay, Jr. Thank you for having my back, never judging me, and being available when I needed a big brother the most. Hope Doughty, I appreciate your service to this country. Salute to you!

<u>Acknowledgments</u>

To my Spiritual Mentors Yolanda Baxter, Ozella Gore, Vernell Gore and Darlene Johnson, I appreciate you for being leaders after God's own heart. Thank you for all the guidance, knowledge, understanding, and Godly wisdom that was bestowed to me. I'm so grateful to be covered and encouraged by each of you.

Psalm 23:4-5 — *"Yea, though I walk through the valley of the shadow of death, I will fear no evil: for thou art with me; thy rod and thy staff they comfort me. Thou preparest a table before me in the presence of mine enemies: thou anointest my head with oil; my cup runneth over."*

Jude 1:24 — *"Now unto him that is able to keep you from falling, and to present you faultless before the presence of his glory with exceeding joy."*

Philippians 4:6-7 — *"Be anxious for nothing, but in everything, by prayer and supplication, with thanksgiving, let your requests be made known to God. And the peace of God, which surpasses all understanding, will guard your hearts and minds through Christ Jesus.*

Contents

<u>Chapter One</u>

Tears of the Righteous

There are no wasted tears for those who trust in God. How many of us feel like we have so much bottled up on the inside that we are in dire need of escape? Your tears are not in vain. This book will provide a fresh perspective on how God wastes none of our experiences. Your tears water the hidden seeds placed on the inside of you that are awaiting to be sprouted out in full effect.

Psalm 126:5-6 NIV tells us: *"Those who sow in tears will reap with songs of joy. Those who go out weeping, carrying seed to sow, will return with songs of joy, carrying sheaves with them."* In this case, your sheaves represent the greatness that God has planted in you to be a difference maker that you will live out and share with the world. God will surprise you beyond your wildest imagination.

After a while, your tears produce something in you that makes you want to get up from that place of defeat. You get tired of finding yourself in places of disappointment, and a hunger starts to arise within you for something different. A burning desire that grows deeper as you wonder how to produce more out of this life. Your tears turn into labor, and your labor, produces a great harvest.

James 1:2-4 NIV tells us: *"Consider it pure joy, my brothers and sisters, whenever you face trials of many kinds because you know that the testing of your faith produces perseverance. Let perseverance finish its work so that you may be mature and complete, not lacking anything."* You don't have to waste your tears. I understand times are hard, but let your pain push you into your purpose. Allow your struggles to build you up so that you can be strong enough to take on whatever comes your way.

The tears that flow from us speak volumes, especially when we can't open our mouths to speak because the pain of life seems unbearable. We won't always understand why we have to go through certain situations. We might even question ourselves and ask what we did to deserve the cards we were dealt. If you find yourself not having any fight left and no more tears to cry, know that God will not leave you alone. He may whisper to our spirit something like, "I have all you need. Just follow Me and I will lead the way."

God provides where He sends.

God uses what we are going through to break the hardness of our hearts. Only He is able to fill us when we are feeling low and empty. Sometimes we are not honest and open with God. For the longest time, I felt afraid to be vulnerable and open up to God. We can have a form of godliness and confess that He is our Lord and Savior, and still be afraid to admit that there is a lack of connection in which oftentimes we feel distant from God. We feel distant because we lack awareness and understanding of how God really feels about us and who he really is.

Saying yes to God is more than just a three-letter word. It is something you feel strongly, deep in your heart. A willingness that you are ready for what lies ahead on your journey is unknown. I pray that this book pushes each of the readers to come into full partnership with God and build a purposeful life. I pray that each reader will feel the

Holy Spirit through my writing, and that God fills each of you with more strategies to persevere and overcome. The first step in taking your tears and producing greatness is to understand that you are victorious and not a victim to your circumstances.

Sometimes when we are in the midst of a storm, we don't understand what God is doing until later, when the storm is over, and the rain has cleared. God loves you, and He doesn't want to hurt or harm you. He is building you up for the great life ahead of you. I pray over each of you as you read this book that you will receive the good while being here in the land of the living and that you will experience the fullness of God's glory right here on Earth.

I hope that each of you will awaken and step out on faith. The key is learning to be content in all circumstances. No matter what life looks like, God deeply cherishes each of you. No one likes to feel less than, forgotten, or worthless. I don't know if anyone has ever told you this, but I want you to know that YOU ARE GOOD ENOUGH.

If your life has started off rough, it can make you doubt yourself and the true worth that's on the inside of you. We can unknowingly define ourselves based on our circumstances. Every day when you wake up, make it a habit to say aloud, "I am good enough." As you hear yourself say it, you will start to believe it.

Right now, you may struggle with receiving God's love. You may feel unworthy of working to-wards a better life for yourself. I'm here to tell you that God will be with you every step of the way. He accepts you, including all your flaws. One thing that you can rest in is that God never changes. He knows the worst about me and all that I have done but yet He redeemed me. He brought me from dried brooks to a wealthy place in His Spirit and He will bring you to a wealthy place in Him as well. He is not a respecter of persons. He treats and loves all of us equally.

We all have experienced a time in life where the brook dried up in certain situations and cir-cumstances because the Lord shifted us to a new place. When the brook dries, it is because it lacks rain. The dried brook indicates that it's time to move from old situations and meet the Lord in a new place that He has prepared for you physically and spiritually.

We are constantly growing and maturing, in constant transition because we were created to change. You can lean on God's love and build your life into something that you will be proud of as He leads you to it. He patiently waits for you to go on adventure with him as you work towards your new life.

I want each of you to understand that God sees you as He created you to be. You have talents and gifts buried deep on the inside of you. I want you to understand that you are a true work of art. God has created you as a priceless masterpiece, and it's time for you to be put on display. Greatness is on the inside of you and it's ready to burst out for the world to see. Your tears were placed in a bottle and God is going to use those same tears to pour out into your life, bringing forth overflow.

Once you surrender your plans and whole self to Him, God will reveal to you a higher purpose for your life that you would only think you could dream of. When you give your mind to God, your imagination flows, bringing the creativity to light that's been on the inside of you. I remember when I started walking in my purpose, I was ready for things to pop off. I thought they would happen automatically. If only it was that easy. I had to learn that it takes time and patience.

There is so much that has to happen before you fully live out what you're working towards. God can speak a word, and we assume that it will happen in an instant. You may go through the opposite of what God promised, but His word to you still stands. A lot may be going on around you, but you have to keep peace within yourself. I know it is hard to have peace when it seems like you keep taking what appears to be losses. God has to subtract what's around you or who is around you that is not of Him, so that more of Him can be presently around you.

For most people, it's going to seem like all hell is breaking loose once you start to actively pursue God's plan. Every day will not be a sunny walk in the park, but even through the storms and rain you will face on your way to greatness, it will make it all worth it. I've never really been fully committed to anything. You know how we can have a habit of starting a goal but not finishing it? We start off pumped up with faith, but when we get into the reality of unexpected challenges, they make what we thought would be an easy goal more challenging.

It's easy to convince yourself, "Oh, this isn't for me because I didn't expect it would take all of this." When the Lord spoke to me in my dreams about the plans He was bringing forth in my life, I had no idea what I would have to overcome. He graciously delivered me from physical sickness, mental agony, abandonment issues, identity confusion, drug dependence, lust, fornication, bisexuality, compulsive eating, and gluttony. I was emotionally shut down and disconnected from everything and everyone around me, including myself. I felt as if my body was here, and I was walking amongst the earth, but my soul was drifting away. My spirit was contrite. Once that deliverance started to take place in me, God was able to move in me as I continually opened myself to him, trusting the process.

In the dream, as God was speaking to me, He showed me a washing machine. I opened the lid of the washer and pulled out a numerous number of books. When I woke up, I wrote my dream down and immediately went into prayer. I didn't realize then what the Lord was saying fully until He blessed me to interpret what the dream meant.

If the mind is willing, the body is able.

There was a major cleaning and purging that had to take place in me before God could pull out what He ordained in my life before the foundation of the world. I had to completely die to myself, so God could revive me and bring me back to life. In my rebirth, an author and a poet were born. I had to allow Christ to lead and as I fully surrendered and submitted.

Life for you may feel like a spin cycle of hurt, disappointment, chaos, grief, instability, and pain. Jesus breaks every demonic cycle and curse and brings forth life, peace, healing, wholeness, forgiveness, hope, encouragement, and a lasting salvation. God speaks to all of us differently. He speaks to us in dreams, visions, in the realm of the Spirit, and sends forth confirmations through His people. Whatever way the Lord has spoken to you about His plan for your life, just trust that He will bring it forth in His timing. There is hope for you. If you've ever wondered, "Do I really have what it takes to dream big and pursue my dreams?" The answer is yes!

I see now what I had to experience was so that others would know they are not alone, and God's hand is mighty and strong to deliver us from anything. We have to remember that God has already gone ahead of us. So, when we start to feel overwhelmed with bringing forth what's on the inside of us, we can run to the one who placed it in us. As we run to God, he fills us with peace and understanding.

Our Heavenly Father tells us in His Word, *"Peace I leave with you; my peace I give you. I do not give to you as the world gives. Do not let your hearts be troubled and do not be afraid* (John

14:27 NIV).” True peace is trusting God, like literally washing your hands of worry and lifting your hands in worship. As you worship, you start to feel lighter. The lighter you feel, the easier it allows you to get back in the game. It is important to take breaks and rest in the presence of God.

The mistake I found myself making was becoming so consumed with thinking I had to accomplish my purpose on my own, which caused a lot of heaviness in my heart. God doesn't want us to be overwhelmed with what He is calling us to. In the midst of the call, it's important to stay humble and reachable. We can be so consumed in works that we become unreachable to God. It's important to go step by step and not look at the whole task itself.

We can't just run or pray ourselves away from the thing we were called to take on.

When you rest under the shadow of the Almighty God, you can focus and break down what comes first. A sound mind produces a productive mind. If the mind is willing, the body is able. Train your mind to be stronger so that thoughts of failure will not come rushing in. God will not let you fail. The enemy makes you think you are powerless, but your trials only increase your anointing. You get to a point where you are not moved by trouble when it comes because God has built you up so high from the things that were meant to destroy you. It may seem as if all things are "failing" around you, and just when you think you have had enough, God will move mountains on your behalf.

We all have inner work that needs to be done. If you find yourself praying your way out of a circumstance, and it seems like that block isn't moving, it's because God wants to use that same "stumbling block" to help build you up. We can't just run or pray ourselves away from the thing we were called to take on.

For a while, it took a lot for me to get back on the righteous path. I had been through some hurtful situations and faced a lot of betrayal. I felt like everyone was out to get me, and I was always on the defense about everything. I had so many people pull on me, take advantage of me, abuse and mishandle me. I felt that there was no point in continuing to do good. My good heart was slowly being plagued by darkness.

Things started to fall into place once I released the people the Lord wanted me to let go of and removed myself from environments that brought death to my spirit. We have to know when to release people. When a season is coming to an end in your life, sometimes it calls for ending certain relationships. Every person isn't always bad, but there is a certain vision that God has, and some people are not meant to go or be where He is leading you to.

I had to let go of people I loved. I still pray for the people I had to release and wish nothing but the best for their lives. As humans we form attachments to people and places and fear letting them go. When you let go of what our Heavenly Father needs you to release to Him, He will release the right resources and people assigned to you.

The storms of life can make you feel like there is no hope or point to living. It may have been a point in life that you even questioned your own existence. Your situations can look dark sometimes, but God steps in, and He will assign people to you to pour into you and lift you up in prayer. God has His Ambassadors of Christ all around us. I actually feel bad for the devil. He makes his plots and schemes, he huffs and puffs, but God wants us to count it as all joy.

I'm excited for each of you as you step out and live in your God-given identity. The more people we have in the light, representing the Kingdom of God, the more darkness can't stand a chance. God really pressed on my heart to add prayers through-out the book that you can lean on in times of un-certainty, doubt, loneliness, a need for connection with Him, and for when you want to praise Him because you're feeling thankful. I hope as you read each prayer that your heart will flutter with love, peace, and assurance from up above.

Chapter Two

Triumph Disguised as Trouble

I've found that when troubled waters are present in our lives, they are designed for us to ride the waves and come out on top. If you don't have the right perspective and understanding of the trouble present in your life, it can cause you to feel like you're drowning. I want to tell you that there is a hidden victory in every troubling situation you face.

Everything we go through has a message behind it. Would you believe me if I told you that there is a golden medallion with your name on it in the midst of that troubling situation, you're in? The more knowledge you have, the more obstacles you can overcome. There is important information hidden in the circumstance you are currently praying your way out of that you need to go to the next level. Whenever you overcome trouble and pass that current test of trial, you gain a badge of honor.

"What you learn from them will crown you with grace and be a chain of honor around your neck." — Proverbs 1:9 NLT

This Scripture refers to learning from your mother and father, but life is our greatest teacher. Trouble means promotion. We look at trouble as a setback and think it's there to destroy us. I want you to know that if you are in deep troubling waters, you have greatness on the inside of you. Trouble is designed to push you to where you need to be. You have to push through and overcome your setbacks. As you overcome and become a willing vessel for God, you will help others come out of their setbacks and allow it to be a set-up for victory.

We need more good in the world, more God in the world. We live in a world that constantly promotes get rich quick schemes, but as an Ambassador of Christ, I encourage you to promote your life as a testimony to others, and let's triumph over the enemy. Too many people are dying, living in depression, and facing suicidal thoughts. We need more healed, whole, and healthy people spreading love and light for the kingdom of God.

The Kingdom of Darkness showboats and promotes itself way too much. Casting itself higher than what it really is. I want you to know that if you feel like you are in the shadows and can't come out of the darkness, know that you are just a mindset shift away from victory. The enemy attacks our minds. Once your mind is gone, it gives the enemy access to take havoc and be in control of your whole life.

As your mindset shifts in Christ, you automatically start helping others before you realize it. When you change, people around you will start to notice and sense a difference in you. As Christ is working on you, you will be able to help uplift and empower the willing people who are connected to you.

Understand though, that it takes time for people to change, so those who knew you before may not want your help. You won't be able to reach everyone, but that doesn't mean you have to dim your light and stop being you. You have to learn not to take things personally, even when you are just trying to help someone. As God has given us grace and mercy, we have to be sure to extend it to others.

Whether we fully understand it or not, it's a spirit that drives our lives and our decision-making. Once we see that it's a spirit that's driving us, causing us to live defeated and depressed lives. We will be more kind to ourselves and stop thinking we are so damaged as an individual. The spirit that is behind depression, defeat, and despair tells us that we are not victorious, that we will be defeated and be in darkness forever.

God calls us up in victory, to mount up with wings like eagles, to soar and be who He created us to be all along. As we grow in God's presence, our desires will change to be more like His. When you feel stuck and don't understand, pray for God to open your eyes and ears spiritually so that you can understand His words to you. Pray for Him to grant you the wisdom on how to set yourself free in Christ, and the strength and courage to go forth to fight the powers of darkness that have been working against your life. When you feel the presence of darkness coming about, you have to fight and cast it down immediately, exalting God higher in your atmosphere, inviting Him into your home, car, workplace, and just about everywhere you go.

When you call out to God continually, He will answer you. Pray for Him to give you the desire to see His goodness in the midst of darkness. He will rescue you and make His presence known to you. He did it for me. I suffered and mentally went through attacks from demonic forces because of warfare and the evil powers of certain enemies surrounding me.

When God opens your eyes and you learn His voice and who He is as a person, you will see that He has been with you all along. Once you learn how to fight back with the Word of God and use your God-given authority, everything has to bow to the name of Jesus and darkness has to flee. Our own mind can make us feel like it's just hell here on Earth. We feel and see the darkness surrounding us, but we have to understand that it can't overtake us.

Growing up, some of you, like myself, may not have had the best circumstances. Constantly moving from house to house and not having a stable environment causes you to have anxiety and gives you a constant feeling like you're unworthy. You go from being a child to an adult, and you never really learn how to function properly in the world because you never took the time to work on childhood traumas. If you grew up not really having a place to call home, it can produce feelings that cause you to believe you don't have a place in this world. You get used to being tossed around, being in one place for a while then having to leave and go somewhere else.

When I was three years old, my mom had a stroke, causing her to be paralyzed on the left side of her body. The stroke also resulted in Aphasia, which is where she lost her ability to speak. She lost the ability to take care of herself and to perform her duties as a mother. The doctors declared that her condition was called Moyamoya disease.

Praise Break

To God be all the glory that she is still living, and the Lord blessed her to live and see her baby girl become an author and poet at 24 years old. I am overwhelmed with God's goodness for preserving both of my parents' lives, so that they could witness what the Lord is doing through me, and there is so much greater in store for my life.

The sickness that struck my mom really traumatized me as a child and caused me to believe that all life was filled with uncertainty. I didn't understand why God would allow that to happen to my mom. Why couldn't I be like other kids and have that motherly experience? I felt abandoned and rejected. I lived in constant fear of disaster happening to me, and I questioned how long it would be before something happened to me.

I was a broken and afraid little girl who had so many questions in my heart and mind, but I couldn't articulate how I was feeling. I was facing feelings and emotions as a three-year-old little girl that a child shouldn't have to think about. I didn't understand how I went from having an apparently healthy mom and staying under the same roof as she took care of me, to being separated without full details or the ability to comprehend all that had happened with her.

Many of us have broken belief systems that were presented to us as children. Everyone is different. Some people have the fear of being killed or being locked up. If you have a parent who went to jail or prison, it can shape your view of what outcome you believe will happen for you. I thank God for changing my beliefs and blessing me with the ability to believe good things concerning my life even at a young age. We don't realize that we are trained to accept fear as a way of life depending on our race, social background and economic status.

I moved to East Arcadia with my dad, which is located in Riegelwood, North Carolina. I was able to finish Pre-K at Sunset Park in Wilmington, North Carolina. I attended East Arcadia Elementary School from kindergarten to fourth grade. I started to settle into country life as a young girl. I had my own four-wheeler, mini motorcycle, and go-kart. I felt like I didn't have any worries when I was riding, and I enjoyed the wind blowing as the dust from the dirt roads clouded around me.

My dad was really strict and displayed tough love. He raised me to his best ability. I didn't know that life for me was about to take another unexpected turn. I got up to go to school, thinking it would be another regular school day. I had a headache that morning in my first period class and couldn't wait for the second period to be over, so I could eat lunch. I made it to my second period class, and it was currently around 9:30-10:30 am.

My teacher was from Jamaica, and everyone loved her. She was known for her accent and her favorite line to say was "Who's that belching in my class?" Kids being kids, we would laugh because no one said belching, we were used to saying burping. The boys in my class being fourth graders, would make themselves burp on purpose, just to get our teacher riled up in excitement.

I remember the day my sun shining school day got interrupted and quickly turned into a nightmare. Deputies raided my dad's garage and his warehouse, which were filled with stolen goods that included weapons, drugs, alcohol, and cash. The news had broken all over East Arcadia about the police kicking in my dad's door. The school got word of what was going on and called me into the office, but I had already gotten word of what happened from my older cousin, who frantically came down the hall to my class to warn me.

She said, "Uncle Carl was in big trouble, and some people are trying to come to the school and take you away!" My heart was pounding, and at each beat, it felt like my heart was falling deeper into my stomach. My dad was on the run for a couple of days before turning himself in. He was charged as a convicted felon, busted for drug distribution and other illegal activities, and was being held on a secured bond of $126,000.

I had never seen so many Durango cars in my life. Undercover police cars swarmed the whole block, and it really scarred my nine-year-old mind. I was so angry and every time I saw a Dodge Durango car, I would get into a rage because all I could think about was the police, who were responsible for attempting to take my dad away and causing such a nightmare in my life. I felt like once again, someone was taking away the life I had once known and the place that was supposed to be home. I knew none of that mattered because they had to do their job and right is right and wrong is wrong. I understood that when you do bad things, you have to pay.

Once again, I had to move. Faced with all these unexpected changes, I was a lost and powerless child. I went into deeper feelings of abandonment. I went back to the city life, switching schools and staying with different family members. Even though I was with family members, it never really felt like home, if that makes sense. There are so many people who come from broken families and unstable backgrounds and wonder if their lives will ever become something. You can still be something even if you feel like you came from nothing.

I'm a witness that your life doesn't have to start as a success story to be a success story. In the real world, we want real results, not just something that's an overnight success. People need the truth for their pain. Someone real to help them see that life is everything but a dream. Through your hard work and dedication, you can fight and have a way out of lack.

There comes a time in life where you have to pick what you will answer to. Will we continue to be known for our past failures and sickness, or will we finish our story with what we want to see? Life has already thrown more than enough at us, so it's time for us to rise, take back our power, throw ourselves back to life, and say enough is enough. You can do anything you put your mind to. You just have to believe and trust in God. Live a submitted life to Him, and He will take you places you would never have been able to go on your own. He will put you in rooms you're not qualified for and make your name great for His name's sake.

You can have a rough start, but a smooth finish. God wants to do great and mighty things through you here in this earthly realm. In Christ Jesus, you get that stability and love you have always longed for. He provides you with a new family and a new way of living. We have our earthly family, but that spiritual family in Christ is one like no other. Being in Christ, you learn how to love yourself, and you give thought to who you give your time to.

When you open your eyes and change your perspective and get a true feel of life, you will see that everything you went through was part of your purpose. We just don't throw away our experiences, we use them to build us up for where God is taking us. You have to kick through the walls of your experiences, tear them down, and rebuild your life on a new foundation. You don't have to wait until your circumstances get better to make a change.

The truth is that we all want someone to save us or discover us. Many people believe they have to wait until things get better, or an opportunity comes along. The problem with this belief is that you don't know when things will get better. That's why you have to create your own opportunities with what you have. Playing it safe is like not playing at all, you have to step out and be willing to make the first move and once you move the other pieces to your success will start to show up to you as God orchestrates it.

You are the answer to how you are going to make it to the top. Do not allow your pain and broken experiences to leave you at the bottom. Use your pain to create your own window of opportunity and climb right to the top, using what was meant to break you down. Don't be afraid to ride that wave because God has already gone before you to straighten everything out.

For a while, I could not keep my head above water. It felt like life was going to take me under. I didn't have any real hope for the future because of my past. I didn't see how anything great could come from me. Before I really got serious with God and started growing into who He created me to be, I tried to handle life in my own hands. This world is tough and hard. You need a higher being than you to help you through. A foundation built without God easily crumbles. His Holy Spirit opens your eyes to so much greatness and gives you a life much better than what you could create alone. Once you build yourself up and have faith in your strong relationship with God, it doesn't matter how scary life's devils may look or what sets itself against you.

Rest assured that God will never let you down. He will never let you go. Trouble doesn't last always. You don't have to gain false security from the world by putting on a show for people. This is a fast-paced, digital world. Everyone posts their good life on social media, but we never see what goes on behind closed doors. We want praise and validation, the likes from others built on something that's not true. Some people don't feel complete unless someone praises them.

It's time we really started to work on ourselves and promote real change and positivity. We have to stop competing with each other and help build each other up. If one person wins, we all win. We have to be willing to break the broken generational ties because times are getting worse and darker. There are too many people dying and getting killed and not caring about where they are going after they leave Earth.

The Hell under the Earth is a different type of hell that you go through on Earth. God cares about our mind, body, soul, and spirit. I know I have been writing about accomplishing and living out your best God-ordained life, but it's more than just success. It's a healing effect that the world needs because people are perishing day by day. The world has preconditioned us to think this is all life is, that we will always be sick, broke, and beat down, which makes some people feel like it doesn't matter where they are going after they die. Your body is going back to dust, but your soul still has to have a place to rest.

The spirit of religion and law has made us feel that we have to perform and be perfect for God to love us and take care of us. We suffer in our shame because we bear the weight of our sin and short-comings. His grace is sufficient for us. Most people don't purposely continue in wrongdoing, but even when we fall, He loves us.

God doesn't want us to run from Him because of the mess we may be in. He desires the best for his children. Our Heavenly Father designed for His remnant to be whole in every area of our lives, not lacking one thing. God always has you in mind (John 3:16). He adores you and takes delight in you (Romans 5:8, Zephaniah 3:17). God wants us to come as we are and for us to believe He will handle the rest. He is the Lord who places a new heart and spirit within us (Ezekiel 36:26). You are not too damaged, difficult, or messed up for God. He can handle you, being that He formed you in your mother's womb (Jeremiah 1:5, Psalm 139:13). Take one step at a time and know that there's no rush. God is patient with us, but the time is now. He is calling us out of the dark.

You were born to shine.

Overcoming our mind, having self-control, and discipline is what we need to walk fully in the light of Christ. Without self-control and self-discipline, you repeat cycles of brokenness. You will be willing to fall for anything and do anything when you are operating out of a broken place. When I first accepted Christ as Lord and Savior, I thought my life with Jesus was going to be great, filled with no problems, and everything would be perfect. From a lack of knowledge and understanding, I used to think really small until I started to study the Word of God.

Believers still go through trials, but the difference is that we go through them in Christ. The Holy Spirit teaches us how to live and navigate our way through it all. Sometimes we think we are too far gone to live a life for God, but while we were sinners, Jesus died for us. The power to overcome and be in the light is already in us. It just takes the right person to bring it out of you.

As I continue to allow my light to shine, I can help others turn on what God has already placed on the inside of them. We don't realize it, but God has placed something on the inside of us that was meant to unlock someone else. Which is why we should never sleep on bettering ourselves and fear change. Each of our lives has value. We all hold the ability to help someone's life become better.

Chapter Three

Building In The Battle

You are a soldier on this battlefield of life, and God wants to supply you with perfect peace. God wants each of you to take hold of Him. As you hold on to Him, He drives out all fear, discouragement, and worry. Our battlefields are in our homes, jobs, schools, grocery stores, our minds, social media and pretty much everywhere you lay your foot to.

The noise of life can be so loud in our ears. Sometimes we might feel like the things around us are too much, and we don't know how we are going to keep going. Jesus often had to separate himself to go pray. His prayer time with God was what kept Him in perfect peace. We need a way of escape from battle, a time to be recharged from how draining life can be. When we don't take a break to meet and sit with God, we miss important instructions.

We can be in battle for so long that we forget to go to the One who trains us for battle. God moves swiftly, and He doesn't always give you the same instructions to fight the battle as He did before. We have to know when to rest in God, so He can take on the hard stuff. We get placed in a battle, and sometimes we can think we are the reason we are winning. We must remember and understand that we are victorious because of the blood of the Lamb and the words of our confession. Knowing that Jesus has already won for you and paid the price for your afflictions takes the edge off.

We tire ourselves out because we don't use the proper weapons in battle. God doesn't move and work as the world does. Which is why we have to seek Him to get instructions on how to overcome what we are facing. The battles we face sometimes feel like they're breaking us. We can feel broken in battle because of the carnal way we fight. The flesh doesn't win in a spiritual battle. We start to look for anything to help us escape from battle. We rely on the things of this world to bring us comfort, but they only comfort us temporarily.

There have been plenty of times, where even as I was writing this book, when I felt burnt out even though I knew it was part of my purpose. Though God was calling me to it, I started to go full force without taking more time to spend with Him. I would pray and have my devoted time with Him, but I found myself writing the book more than I was spending time with Him. Luckily, I received His message at the right time.

He instructed me to rest in His presence because major changes were about to take place. I discovered that as I paused and pressed in His presence, He led me to Scriptures that would help me when I was stuck. I can admit that as I was writing, I felt myself feeling overwhelmed at times because I wasn't allowing His spirit to lead me. I was working from a place of anxiety.

It's a process and there are steps we have to take before we can walk fully into what He has for us. Writing this book taught me that if we get too caught up in doing, we can miss what really needs to be done. I found some of my best inspiration when I drove places, parked my car, and allowed God to speak to me based on what was happening around me.

Humor is also an important part of battle. God knows that things can get rough and just how real they can get for us. So, when He does things to make me smile and laugh, no matter how simple they may seem, it shows He cares about us being happy. In battle, we don't have to be tense and always on edge. When we wait on the Lord and follow His guidance, we learn to relax.

In the wait, we learn to depend on Jesus. The Lord shines bright, and He has a way of speaking to us that we can't miss Him. As the Lord causes His face to shine on us, He brings peace and clarity. It's important to have an open mind and know that every encounter with God is an adventure because you never know what to expect.

As the days go on, we start to feel like we are running out of time. The battlefield of life doesn't feel like a smooth transition. Life always feels busy. Even in the midst of busyness, we have to learn to slow down and set time apart to make sure we are still in God's flow. God wants us to be under His flow. The enemy makes us think that we have to rush to accomplish what God has set for us. God still cares about us taking care of ourselves and, most of all, taking time out for Him.

The enemy wants us to be prideful and to feel like we don't need God. The enemy desires for us to work without God, when the truth is we can't get far without God. God had to humbly remind me that, ultimately, He is the One who causes things to happen. Don't get so caught up in your own work that you mess up the flow of how He wants to bring His promise to pass.

He may assign us to a purpose, but He has the ultimate guide on how to provide what's needed. Life's circumstances are meant to build character. The characteristics that we need: patience, kindness, obedience, attentiveness, willingness, faithfulness, perseverance, love, humility, and integrity are in Christ. We need true Godly character for what He is establishing in us to run smoothly.

A bird has wings, and the bird knows it was made to fly, but it always knows when it's time to take a rest on a branch or to come back down to ground level. In your downtime, when things start to slow down and you come to a resting point, it allows you to prepare for the next shift that's coming.

Maybe you haven't given your life to Christ yet, or you fell off the narrow path, and you feel like you don't have what it takes for the battle of life or even how to start living for God. I want you to know that God can still fulfill His purpose for your life. It may look gloomy in your life right now, but in those gloomy days you will learn the most valuable lessons that are meant to help you bring your own sunshine to cloudy days.

Sometimes we need the storms of life to cleanse us, nourish us, and to set our lives on the path it's supposed to be on. Of course, we know every day cannot be sunny, but the rain that comes in our lives is to help us grow. When the weather changes in our life, we can tend to base our peace off of the rainbows and sunshine, but not when the clouds and storms settle in.

God teaches us to have peace and joy in all circumstances. We go through losses in life. We lose people, money, jobs, time, houses and just about anything that once held much value to us. Our losses teach us not to be too comfortable. Sometimes we have to get shaken up and rained on to grow. For every loss, it's a gain to go deeper within yourself and grow at a different level than where you were previously. When we lose people, it's hard because it's a subtraction from our lives.

People who pass away mean the world to us, or we just grow out of relationships with people. Sometimes we feel like we take losses at the wrong time, but we cannot control when we lose things. As life goes on, we learn how to still win when we take unexpected losses. We learn how to keep rowing our boats. Losses are meant to make us grow closer to our Creator. God wants our attention, and we miss His calls because we are either unaware that he is calling or just not ready to pick up the phone to answer Him.

Our losses get our attention. When we lose something, it brings us to a place of surrendering to the Most High. Our losses teach us that we have someone greater to answer to, and we can't do life alone. When you are in a tough circumstance, it's not easy to see your way out. Things can appear to be rocky, and we don't understand what God is doing, but we have to just trust His timing. God is not a man who shall lie. He is our strength in times where we need to be uplifted.

When you're at your weakest,
you can trust in Jesus.

It's times when life feels so hard that you don't feel like getting out of bed to go to work or even to the grocery store. Knowing that you have responsibilities and people to take care of, so you draw your strength from up above and push to keep going. We lose the things of this world, people, and our possessions, but God teaches us that He will never leave us nor forsake us. We get dependent on the things of this world and forget that God is here. Ultimately, He is our first love, above all things.

There is an appointed time for everything. His love is perfect, and when one door closes, another door opens. We may not see it with our physical eyes. Faith helps us see with our spiritual eyes. We have to go through the valley to see the true light we really hold. Sometimes we find gratification from the things of this world and base our security on outside pleasures. You learn after a while that God has been carrying you all along.

You see how strong you were without that thing you were once so dependent on before you lost it. God's presence is mighty and will fill every void you may be missing through whatever loss you may be facing. God fills you up and provides security for you in your time of need. He teaches you to stand on him so that if you ever face another loss, you know you have gained more of God to provide for you.

Prayer for the Battlefield

Dear God, I thank You for the plans that You have for my life. I also know the enemy has plans for my life too. Thank You, Jesus, that you are the greatest power, and I can never be defeated because of the weight and glory of Your Name. Though the enemy wants to steal, kill, and destroy, I know that You came to give me life and to supply it more abundantly. The devil may try to whisper in my ear and tell me that I am nothing, but I know I am more than a con-queror in Christ Jesus. God, I will choose to listen to Your voice and follow you.

God, I pray for a fresh outpour of Your Holy Spirit over my life as I put Your Words into action to seek you daily and receive my spiritual food in Your Holy Word. When the enemy wants to come against my freedom and healing that only You provide for me. Jesus, may I always remember it's by Your unmerited favor that I am freed and healed. It's by Your grace Lord, that I can stand. Not by my own doing but by what You accom-plished at Calvary. Change my perspective, Lord, on how I view every battle that is placed in my court. Bless me to have a heav-enly perspective on life's challenges.

When thoughts arise and tell me that I will be destroyed and won't make it out, may I be quick to cast it down, all imaginations in

Jesus' name. I proclaim victory over my life because You go before me and make the crooked paths straight. Grant me the grace to speak only words of healing over myself, confessing that by Jesus' stripes I am healed. Help my unbelief. Lord thank You for freeing me from sin and death, releasing me from the authority of darkness. In Jesus' name. Amen.

Chapter Four

Miracle in Motion

In the motion of life, tragedy strikes. Although my body had taken an unexpected strike of sickness, it didn't know I was in store for a move of God to show forth what it means to be healed by Jesus' stripes. What tragedy are you currently facing in your life that you are hoping to see a miracle of God take place? What started off as an inflammatory skin disorder quickly started to turn into an array of chills, nausea, headaches, fatigue, and weariness. I started to get patches of dry skin, and it would become itchy and red.

Eczema ran on both sides of my family, so I thought the dry skin was common. As the weeks went by, my body started to swell rapidly. My doctors were worried that this was turning into something more serious than atopic dermatitis.

I was starting to show symptoms of heart failure. I was always tired, and when I did sleep, I would wake up feeling breathless. I had trouble breathing when I laid down, and I felt like I was suffocating. I had to sleep with my body elevated, sitting up because I was afraid that I would not make it through the night without gasping for air. I needed a breathing machine to help me breathe.

My skin was like a memory foam pillow. Imagine pressing your hand down on a pillow and seeing your print as it rises back up. The swelling in my body turned into pitting edema. My legs, ankles, and feet were easily indented. That's how inflamed my skin was from the fluid buildup. Oozing edema started to form past my knees, down to my feet. My skin was weeping, literally.

I had to wear compression socks that came all the way up to my knees to help with the inflammation. The compression socks were supposed to help with blood flow from my legs to my heart. I couldn't wear my regular size 8 shoes because of the swelling. It seemed as if my feet had turned into the size of a bear paw. The only thing that would fit and be comfortable for my feet were cushioned bedroom shoes. My body was under so much stress that it would overheat, and I would become dizzy, but I would feel cold.

Every time I ate, it would just come right back up. Then I would lose my appetite and not want to eat because of the constant vomiting. Months went by and I wasn't getting better. I had exhausted my care with my doctors, they felt I needed more skilled professional care. That could possibly give me more answers and the help I needed. My primary care sent me to the University Hospital in Chapel Hill.

After the intensive tests were run, I had options to choose from for treatment and medications that would help my condition, both topical and oral. The doctors from Chapel Hill shared the results with my doctors back in Wilmington and felt that I could receive treatment at their facility. My next step was to start Light Box Therapy and UVB treatment at Wilmington-Midtown Health Dermatology. My eczema had worsened on top of what was already going on with my heart and the edema in my lower body.

My care team was the best. They were so positive and uplifting during this time of my life. They called me "sunshine," and always complimented my smile and told me how they saw a great future ahead of me. They would say, "Ms. Doughty, you're going places. We see it in you, you brighten up our day with every doctor visit." With all I was going through, all I could do was smile. I smiled with tears in my eyes. I smiled even when pain was lying deep inside.

I was able to have a well experienced doctor who clinically specialized in acne, skin cancers, rashes, skin lesions, and mole removal. My phototherapy experience using the UVB light treatment started to be too harsh for my skin. Though I wore sunscreen, it didn't stop me from getting burned by the light. I just kept praying because I knew the UVB therapy was too strong for my sensitive skin. My skin was constantly shedding, which caused discoloration from the burns of the UVB light.

I was worn out from the constant doctor visits for treatment. I cried out to God. I wanted answers. I wanted to understand why I was facing this at such a young age. It felt like my heart was giving out on me. The Lord heard my cry and answered quickly. I was able to see the plans the enemy had for me, but God showed me the might of His word. I was instructed to continue to take my oral and topical medications and to pray.

When you have been praying for months or however long, and you want to see instant results, doubt can easily creep in, causing disbelief that God would move on your behalf. If something doesn't come as fast as you want it, don't give up. If you just keep holding on, God will see you through and bless you double for holding on and being faithful to Him in prayer and worship. Continue to thank Him for all He has done and bless His name. At the right time, God will come through. He is never too early or late.

Things are getting better for you,
trust in God's timing.

I spoke these words over my body daily: "By Jesus' stripes I'm healed." I had no more fight left in me, and I had no other choice but to believe that God would heal me because of His Word. I prayed for God to stabilize my heart, and for my organs to function properly. I prayed for healthy blood flow and circulation throughout my whole body.

God allowed me to see the plans the enemy had for my life. I had a dream about my mother, and I being tied and bound down sick in a hospital bed. I knew that I had to continue to lean on God like never before. The enemy had plans to strike my life with sickness and untimely death, but God said I shall live and not die (Psalm 118:17). God used my life to show the doctors and others around me that He is in the miracle business. That when we speak a thing and believe with all our might, it shall be so. God blessed me to lay hands on myself and healing took place in the name of Jesus. God wants to do the same for you.

Giving honor to God, who is the head of my life. I am edema free right now. I no longer have to wear compression socks, and I'm able to fit back into my regular shoes. I can breathe on my own without a breathing machine, my heart is now pumping blood and my body is healthier than it has ever been. God is able to cure every incurable disease. He is the ultimate healer. We have to stay focused on God and not the storm. No matter what tragedy strikes, believe with all your might that God can turn any situation around.

When everyone else is against you, know God is always for you.

The vision that God has for our lives is heavenly peace, healing, and wholeness. God is calling us to be in partnership with Him. We create a partnership with God when we trust Him to bring us through the most troubling circumstances, even when we don't see a way out. It's a miracle that God allowed me to live through the exact thing that was supposed to take me out. I'm so grateful that my body is fluid free, and I can function on my own.

When things get hard, we can tend to get mad at God and run from Him. We blame Him for the pain and tragedy that happens. A lot of people feel like if God is in control of everything, why does He allow bad things to happen to people? Get into God's presence in order to hear from Him. He longs for all of us to commune with Him. Ask God for wisdom, knowledge, and understanding. He will surely give it to you.

Having an authentic vision matters. No matter what the test results say or how long the doctor may predict how long you have to live, God has the last and final day. When you start to believe and have faith, it's going to be tested by trials, but you can't give up on the vision God gives you. Don't limit your vision based on the negative circumstances you are currently experiencing. What your life looks like now may not align with where you want to go in life, but where you are currently doesn't have to define how your life will be forever.

In order to have vision, you have to have discipline. Without a vision, people will perish (Proverbs 29:18). You have to know where you are going. When you don't have a vision, you will be more likely out here doing anything with anybody at any place. It's important to have something to look forward to. Seeing all this stuff going on in the world can be discouraging, and it can take a toll on you mentally.

The time is now for fresh leadership to arise. You can start right where you are now. When you step out and break the cycles of fear and unbelief by doing the exact thing you are afraid of doing, you help build others' tenacity in the midst of adversity. The time for creativity is now. God is speaking to us through the catastrophes going on in the world. When you are the Lord's very own, you don't have to worry about anything. Trust him to provide for everything you have your hands building to do. By holding yourself accountable, you will stay disciplined and focused.

Prayer for Healing

Lord, I thank You for the opportunity to be totally Yours. All that I am belongs to You. I thank You for making the devil out of a liar by raising me up again from the grave of death. I praise You for raising me up from deadly circumstances. Jesus, I pray for Your blood to cover every area of my life. I need all of me covered by Your precious blood. May a fresh praise rise in me, so that You can get the glory You deserve.

Lord grant my doctors fresh wisdom for my condition. I thank You in advance for the best care. Orchestrate the minds of every health care provider that they would be of great service to me. I thank You for blessing my body with heavenly supernatural healing. I declare and decree that my body is well because I have the DNA of Heaven within me.

Lord, I thank You for the courage to step out in boldness right in the face of adversity. Bless me to have the belief and mindset to believe that I can never be defeated. Help me to remember that my Savior is greater than any sickness. I pray for my body to function in the way you created it to function. In the name of Jesus, I pray, Amen.

Chapter Five

A Small Voice

The loudest person in the room isn't always the toughest, and the quietest person in the room isn't always the weakest. Be careful how you treat and speak to people. We know and understand the effect of what we put out into the atmosphere; we get back. The bridges you burn matter. The same bridge you thought you would never have to cross again is the one you may need to get to the other side. The person you overlook and push to the side is the same person God will use for His glory. As soon as you think you don't need someone, the tables turn, and you end up trying to come back to the one you did wrong.

God allowed me to see the intentions certain

people had towards me, yet I still had to show love and kindness. Some people are placed in our lives as a test. We are meant to help each other grow. Be mindful of how you treat someone when it seems like they are in a time of need. Just because someone is down and out right now, that doesn't mean it's over for them. We all go through seasons in life, and some are harder than others. Matthew 5:5 NIV tells us, *"Blessed are the meek they will inherit the earth."* A small voice produces a mighty move.

Start respecting people who most people take for granted. You never know who you may need down the line, or what situation you may find yourself in. Keep up the good work; it won't be long until you see everything fall into place and work in your favor. It's just a series of tests we have to go through to make sure we don't fold, we don't change who we are, and to make sure we have the right character for the type of blessings we are asking for. A lot of people misuse the blessings that God has given them, a lot of people have gotten greedy and have not used what God has given them to help and bless others. Yes, take care of yourself, but don't forget other people.

In Ephesians 4:1-2, the Apostle Paul gives this charge: *"Therefore I, a prisoner for serving the Lord, beg you to lead a life worthy of your calling, for you have been called by God. Always be humble and gentle. Be patient with each other, making allowance for each other's faults because of your love."* It's easy for us to be gentle and kind to the people we like and who seem to like us, but the true test comes when we have to face people who may be more difficult. I'm not saying that you are supposed to allow people to walk all over you and treat you any kind of way, but when it comes to having interactions with people, we have to practice self-control and establish proper boundaries.

You know how it is when you have an interaction with someone, and it seems like they suck the life out of you. That interaction is over, but you are still harboring and holding on to it because it's in your mind, constantly replaying. When a person or thing has your mind, it has you forever, until you make a decision to let go. Remember, it is God's job to handle people who hurt you. You want to keep your hands clean and just pray for people, that God would change their hearts to love like Christ. It's not worth letting someone have control over you because it causes built up anger and resentment.

God extends much grace and mercy to everyone. He loves and treats us with gentleness in spite of our long list of sins and flaws, which makes it somewhat easier for us to love one another in spite of all that has been done. Sometimes we can't hear God and make room for what He wants to bring into our lives because we want to hold on to the past.

It's important not to focus so much on the fall, but how you rise. It's easy for us to focus on our mistakes and not the progress we have made. Embrace where you are, but don't get stuck. It's about being honest and coming out of the mindset of unbelief. When things feel unknown or uncomfortable, I'm not always happy about it. To keep myself from complaining, I thank the Lord for seeing me through every uncomfortable situation. I asked Him to help me grow and become a better person. Give thanks in all things, because victory today is YOURS.

Prayer For Hearing God's Voice

God, I praise You and lift Your name up. Thank You, Jesus, for providing a way for me to our Heavenly Father (John 14:6). Help my heart remember that whatever I ask in Your name, Jesus, it will be given unto me, if it's according to our Father's will (John 14:13). Bless my ear gates to be sensitive to You Lord. Increase my awareness of

Your sweet heavenly voice. Remove every desire in me that is blocking us from communicating. Every hindrance designed to make me spiritually deaf, burn it with Your Holy Fire.

Heavenly Father, I ask that You cancel out all monitoring spirits from out of my territory. Bless my feet to go forth into heavenly territories. Every voice in my life that tries to be louder than Yours. God, would you mute them out? Remove the lying echoes of the enemy. I bind every spirit of replay and backwardness from my life. Peace is my portion for the rest of my life.

I pray for forwardness and longevity in my camp. I am covered from every evil dart and wile of the enemy because of the protective armor of God. Heavenly Father, I ask that You be my comfort when I'm feeling comfortless, my voice when I'm feeling voiceless, my shield when my soul feels like it's aching and my friend when I feel like I have no one to run to. In Jesus' name, I pray, Amen.

Chapter Six

The Table is Set

This book is about me telling my story, but I dedicate this chapter to ALL OF YOU. I had you in mind as I wrote this book. Your story is just as important as mine. God is patient with us, and He won't force himself on us. There is a door placed between us and the Lord. His side is always open. He longs for us to keep the door of our heart and whole being open for Him to flow in freely. A sincere heart and a desire for closeness with God are the keys to an atmosphere of worship.

A lot of the moments I had with the Lord when I was weak and deep in the pit of despair weren't long or fancy prayers. They were short and sincere prayers. To be honest, a lot of times I would have to call on the name of Jesus and say, "Lord, I'm trusting You to save me from this constant feeling of heaviness."

We have to be willing to wait on God while He paves the way.

In a sense, what you overcome becomes your gift to encourage someone else. It's a lot of us who are coming up against a lot of opposition in our health, finances, family, and just life in general. It's easy to think negatively. Sometimes God will allow things to come in our path to keep us on our toes. We get comfortable in this world and forget that we have an enemy of our soul. Any ungodly thing is against our soul.

Never give the enemy the satisfaction of seeing you defeated. God's strength alone brings us through things we never thought we could over-come. The bigger the attacks and battles you face, the bigger your blessings from the Lord. Once you seek God and repent of your sins. It may not make sense why we have to go through so much hard-ship, but when we go through it, what's on the oth-er side is much sweeter. Some people never make it to the table because they think the opposition in the storm is their final destination.

What we don't know is that there is a table prepared for us behind the hard times. Your enemies are not always people. Your enemy could be sickness, addiction, depression, financial hardships, or anything that burdens you. When you invite God into your life, He steps in and says let me bring you through this. We have to be willing to wait on God while He paves the way. God allows the enemy to attack us because of our sinful nature. The attacks are meant for us to yield to God (Read the story on Job). A double portion is restored to us after the enemy's attack.

Wait on God to position you where
He wants you to be.

I also thank the family members that talked about me and said I wasn't going to make it through college and that I would only end up pregnant and not finish school. By the grace of God, He let the exact opposite happen. I was able to complete my four-year studies at Fayetteville State University, receiving a bachelor's degree in psychology with a minor in criminal justice.

Some people will try to project their feelings onto you. People didn't expect me to go far because of my mom's sickness and my dad's being incarcerated. The projection of others' opinions on how they want you to turn out can be so negative and degrading. Sometimes others will expect less of you because all they see is less for themselves. People would rather speak words of death to you than to speak life to you.

Every bad thing ever spoken to me only contributed to the growing pains that birthed my greatness. The point of me saying all this is that no matter what you go through, how you view your opposition is important. Let God do the talking for you, as he elevates you in the face of those who cursed you. All God wants us to do is rest in him. Even witchcraft can't hold those who belong to God down. People can't define your life. Sometimes you need that betrayal. You need that pain to push you into purpose. When you are under God's wing and protection, there is nothing anybody can do to stop the plan of God.

There were many mornings when I woke up with headaches that lasted for hours, sometimes all day. I had sleep interrupted nights because of the torrents of heavy rain pouring through my troubled mind. I felt like a thundering dark cloud of anxiety was the constant aftermath of the day after worry alarmed my heart by its sounds of terror. Our worst circumstances are for others to believe in us again, including ourselves. In order to be restored, you have to be broken. What appears to be bad is just showcased that way, so when Jesus brings you out, He gets all the credit and is glorified.

We reject God's best because when it comes, sometimes it looks like the worst. Part of becoming God's evidence is literally what it sounds like. The Holy Spirit will shape you into all He created you to be as you continue to walk with God. To be emptied out from the world is necessary in order for the Lord to mold you into the masterpiece He always designed you to be. The molding and shaping doesn't always feel good. It comes with ups and downs. It is filled with emotions and wounds from the past being exposed just so that you can be restored. When the Lord redeems us, it's already done and paid in full by the finished work of Christ and the blood He shed for us. As we grow closer to Him and study His Word our minds are transformed as we live out our redemption.

<u>All About You</u>

I have placed some motivational scriptures of God's promises that you can hold on to. My personal scriptures are Isaiah 41:10 and Joshua 1:9. The next couple of pages are for you to pour your heart out to God. Before you start your prayer, think of your personal scriptures that you read when you need motivation. Write it out and meditate on it for as long as you need. In what ways are you expecting God to move in your story?

1. _____

_____

_____

_____

_____

_____

_____

_____

_____

_____

_____

2. _____

_____

_____

_____

_____

_____

_____

_____

_____

3. _____

_____

_____

_____

_____

_____

_____

_____

_____

_____

_____

4. _____

_____

_____

_____

_____

_____

_____

_____

_____

_____

_____

_____

_____

_____

5. _____

_____

_____

_____

_____

_____

_____

_____

_____

_____

_____

_____

Motivational Bible Verses

Proverbs 3:5-6 ESV: Trust in the LORD with all your heart, and do not lean on your own understanding. In all your ways acknowledge him, and he will make your paths straight.

Psalm 23:1 ESV: The LORD is my shepherd; I shall not want.

Psalm 23:5 NIV: He prepares a table before me in the presence of my enemies. He anoints my head with oil; my cup overflows.

1 John 1:9 ESV: If we confess our sins, he is faithful and just to forgive us our sins and to cleanse us from all unrighteousness.

1 Peter 5:7 ESV: Casting all your anxieties on him, because he cares for you.

Matthew 6:11 ESV: Give us this day our daily

bread.

2 Thessalonians 3:3 ESV: The Lord is faithful, who will establish you and guard you from the evil one.

Isaiah 12:2 NIV: God is indeed my salvation; I will trust and won't be afraid. Yah the Lord, is my strength and shield; he has become my salvation.

John 3:16 NIV: For God so loved the world that He gave His one and only Son, that whoever believes in Him shall not perish but have eternal life.

Personal Prayer

_____

_____

_____

_____

_____

_____

_____

_____

_____

_____

_____

_____

_____

_____

_____

_____

_____

_____

_____

_____

_____

_____

_____

_____

_____

_____

_____

_____

_____

_____

_____

_____

Chapter Seven

Divinely Aligned

Satan wants to keep people in the cycle of defeat. Defeat is the opposite of victory. It only serves one purpose, and that is to distract you. The devil wanted me to continue to be confused about myself and keep me in a state of questioning my identity. Satan sent a lady into my life who came and spoke a word that was heavily cursed to me. Her words to me were that my family and friends were going to put me in a mental institution.

The word the lady spoke to me didn't align with God's Word or His plans for my life. Any word spoken to you or over you that doesn't align with the Word of God, you have to bind up and cast down immediately in the name of Jesus. How do you bind up a word curse? To bind up word curses, speak God's Word over yourself and forbid the curses from happening. Fear feeds the enemy, and subconscious fear feeds the conscious. What we are aware of or sensitive towards acts as a control factor in our lives. We tend to allow the fear of what ifs to control our lives, and the reality is most of our what ifs never happen.

For example, I had to face betrayal from people I never expected. I was hurt badly by people I trusted. The Holy Spirit prophetically led me through the mental attacks I was going through. I learned the power of praise and worship. I had to pray and fast intensively so that I could be focused and see what the Lord was showing me. God showed me the faces in the realm of the Spirit of my family members who wanted to choke out my destiny. The job of the python spirit was to keep me stagnant and not go forward with the call God had on my life. It was a curse put on me that I would go mentally insane. The Lord blessed me to be able to see the witch who was responsible for conjuring up the mental madness that was taking place in my life.

Jealous spirits were at play through specific family members. I went through months battling with the spirit of insanity, suicidal thoughts, and attempts at untimely death from evil spirits sent to take my life. People think God is stupid, that the works done in the dark won't be revealed. If I could describe the demonic spirit God allowed me to see, I would describe it as a slender black spirit shaped as a snake that was trying to choke me as I would sleep at night and when I would drive my car.

Spiritual satanic devices are real, and people joke as if this isn't real until it happens to them. Then they don't know what hit them. God blessed me with strong prayer warriors, women mighty in His Spirit, to pray for me. My spiritual mentors in the Lord were able to see what I couldn't see in the Spirit to help bring me clarity towards my deliverance from the attacks of the enemy. Jesus had mercy on me and brought me back to life. God showed me there is nothing impossible for Him to do.

People are suffering from witchcraft sent by enchanters and diviners, and they don't understand what's happening to them. If you believe in God, He can cancel out the power of the enemy. God has more power than the enemy does. If you find yourself in a similar experience like I went through, read Psalm 16 for the confidence that the Lord will deliver you from every evil plot against your life. Psalm Chapter 17 is a prayer for protection from every witchcraft, hindering and monitoring spirit. Psalm Chapter 18 is for praising God for delivering you from the hands of the enemy.

God delivered me and I made it out so that I can testify to other people around the world who may be going through similar circumstances. This experience taught me how to forgive. I learned the power of Mark 16:18 NIV, *"they will pick up snakes with their hands; and when they drink deadly poison, it will not hurt them at all; they will place their hands on sick people, and they will get well."*

God used this experience to help me train for spiritual warfare. I trusted that God would not let the word of the enemy spoken over my life come true. If I had given up on God and believed this experience would send me to a mental institution, there is no telling where I would be now. What was designed to kill me, pushed me into my destiny. The attacks I faced allowed me to give birth in the spirit to what God had in mind to bring forth in my life.

Family knows more about you than strangers. Certain family and friends who are around you can tend to be envious and jealous of you. People you least expect will do things to hurt you the most. When someone doesn't want to see you happy, they will do all they can to make sure you're unhappy. They will distract you in every way they can to keep you from prospering. They fear you will do better than them.

Some people will stop at nothing to see you destroyed. Mean spirited people will see the good in you and will do everything to tear you down so that you can't see the good within yourself. As long as you are doing what they want and their manipulation tactics are working on you, everything is fine. But as soon as you start to stand up for yourself and call them out, they try to play like you're crazy and don't know what you're talking about.

People will use you to make themselves look good and when they are done with you, they chew you up and spit you out. We are likely to trust the people we know over a stranger. A stranger will come to your aid and rescue you quicker than your family members so as Hebrews 13:2 says, "Do not neglect to show hospitality to strangers, for thereby some have entertained angels unaware."

God wants every Believer to become a house of faith and a house of prayer. We do this by presenting our bodies as temples unto the Lord. This allows us to draw closer to God when we face attacks of wickedness. Things may attack us, but God allows us to move about, allowing our blood to flow and us to walk on our enemies. How do we expect to use the authority God has given us if we are not placed in situations to train us to grow stronger? I used to allow myself to be so burned out and off focus by every little distraction that came in my path. I wanted things to be easy and to flow, but at any disruption, I allowed myself to be interrupted.

Don't render evil for evil.

I thank God for blessing me with endurance in Him. That I would be encouraged to acknowledge him above every sin, sickness, emotion, circumstance, trial and tribulation, every form of despair, unworthiness, confusion, doubt, unbelief, and uncertainty. I learned not to be disrupted by the tactics of the enemy by calling on the name of Yahweh. I made sure I had up close and personal thanksgiving experiences with God daily. Constantly acknowledging His presence and sovereignty over every dart being thrown at me. I pursued God with intentionality to make Him my dwelling place everywhere I go. My spiritual mentor Vernell always tells me "Lil Sis, the enemy wants to wear the saints out and we all need a covering spiritually. If no one else covers you, know I'm always covering you in prayer."

Prayer for Heavenly Alignment

God, I ask that You lift the curse off of every helpless soul. Thank You Jesus for opening the eyes of the blind so that Your people can see the truth. Help us to see the enemy from afar and up close. We welcome the Holy Spirit to come into our lives. Deliver us from every evil thought, every evil spirit, and every evil way.

Bless our steps to be aligned with You, Heavenly Father. Keep our feet from walking in any curse that has been sent to destroy us. Forgive us for getting off the righteous path to life. Bring us back to You, Oh Elohim, The Holy One, creator of Heaven and Earth. Break the yokes of destruction which leads to death. Thank You Jesus for cutting the cords of evil root workers and changing their hearts to commune and worship You, the Only True Living God. May your Heavenly Angels continue to bear us up from any deadly accidents and for your Holy Blood to cover every area of our lives. In the name of Jesus, Amen.

Chapter Eight

The Freedom to Move Forward

What part of your past is keeping you from moving forward? Are the invisible chains of regret, shame, and guilt currently keeping you down? The road to freedom is forgiveness. What haven't you forgiven yourself of? I'll share my story with you about how the chains of who I used to be were holding me down. It was a time in my life that I wasn't fully giving myself over to God. I was holding on to the hurt I had experienced when I didn't receive love from the people who were supposed to love me. I buried my hurt and internalized everything. I blamed myself for how people treated me, taking on the responsibility of someone else's actions.

During that time, I didn't love myself and my self-esteem was low. I was trying to find myself through other people, but I only lost the part of me I thought I did know. I "needed" validation to feel secure. I was held down by the approval of others. I realized I had been looking for me all along. I had to lose myself to find myself again. I found out I had to separate and learn how to be by myself. You can't force anyone to love you. Before I found it to be true that in Christ, I was made complete according to Colossians 2:10, it was a rude awakening I had to undergo.

On your worst day, remember you're still a child of God.

I had my Bible in one hand and my other hand was in the world. I feared how others would receive me based on who they knew me to be in the past. I allowed my worldly identity to take away from my identity in Christ. I knew that God wanted me to go forth and use me for His purposes, but I wasn't ready to let go of what was making me "feel good." The sin that I was in felt good. I enjoyed it and used it as a "protective barrier." The truth is the sin was only serving as a barrier between me and God. I wanted to live a fast life.

I opened the door to sex and drugs as a way to heal my pain. I enjoyed the sexual connection and affection I received. I didn't feel like I deserved better, so I never demanded it. Deep down, I wanted better, but I felt unable to receive it. I was able to love and care for people and do right by them, but I struggled to receive love. I became unavailable and just wanted a connection, even if it was sexual and temporary. I protected myself by numbing how I really felt because I didn't want to feel anything.

This world taught me how to pretend, so I learned how to get by. When you grow up in households or environments where you can't express yourself, it's not a normal thing to do. Culture adapts to a way of pretending like there's nothing wrong. You learn how to suppress your emotions when you feel like you don't have anyone you can trust or who understands you. I knew how to make it look like I had it all together, but deep down I was shattered. Shattered from my pain, disappointments, abandonment issues, hopelessness, addictions, sexuality, and lack of confidence.

Pain can lead you to places that cause you more pain. The pain led me to places I had no business being. Even then, the Lord was communicating with me. God had unsaved people to give me a message that He pressed on their hearts.

I didn't listen. I ignored God, which only pushed me further into the pit of despair. Strangers would come and say the same thing God had already spoken to me about. Yet, God didn't give up on me, and I'm so thankful for His faithfulness. He'll send a message to you through other people. He demonstrates clearly what He wants us to know.

He allowed some of the people I was smoking and hanging with to say, "this lifestyle ain't for you," "you don't look like the type to be doing this," "you have so much potential to do something with yourself and I can tell by the way you talk and carry yourself that you are smart." I didn't believe in myself, and I enjoyed the thrill of the situationships I was in. I was very adventurous and just wanted to fill the emptiness that I was feeling on the inside. I've had dealings with people I knew were in relationships.

I've done things I'm not proud of and been to places I know I didn't belong. I had a place where I could go smoke, have some drinks, and give private dances. I could make the experience that I wanted, and it didn't have to become intimate, just tease. God quickly proved to me that He is my provider and that I don't have to seek my own way of getting what I need by taking matters into my own hand.

He kept me from being shot, stabbed, and choked until I was unconscious. Even when I was out, he kept me protected in his arms. I was walking into the open doors of the grave, but God quickly shut that door and brought me to a doorway of life. I've been in situations that felt like I was in a movie. God has been my protector all along. The night I'm about to describe had become a nightmare.

After a night of partying downtown, around 1 am, plans for the night changed. Marie, Kaia, Nikita, and I left to go with Quan, Marie's boyfriend, and his two friends, ZJ and Anthony to a chill spot. For obvious reasons, there have been some name changes as requested for confidentiality. We were down with going because Marie "trusted" Quan, and I had seen Anthony around a few times, and ZJ was Quan's right-hand man.

When we got to the spot, Quan and Anthony started to roll more blunts, while ZJ did a couple lines of cocaine and threw back two shots and a beer. Nikita had taken some pills. Kaia, Marie, and I were already drinking and finishing up the blunts we were already smoking. Music was playing, and we were all vibing and in the zone. The guys were playing pool until Marie, and I started dancing. Kaia was already messed up from the drugs she had taken on top of drinking more alcohol.

After a while, Kaia had to go to the bathroom and insisted we let her go by herself because she didn't want to stop our little show, as she called it. Quan's right-hand man, ZJ nodded his head, telling him to come over that way. They exchanged words, then dapped each other up. I could tell Quan had given ZJ the go ahead to try Kaia.

I knew something wasn't right because Kaia had just left to use the bathroom, and I noticed ZJ had been eyeing her the whole night. He waited about two minutes before leaving to go out from where everyone was chilling at. Before we knew it, Kaia started screaming, "STOP, I SAID NO!!" repeatedly followed by a cry for help. She thought she wasn't going to be heard over the music we were dancing to. It was clear what was going on.

When Nikita and I were walking towards the back to go help Kaia, we got pulled back and told to sit down and chill because there was nothing going on. I was praying, asking the Lord to let all of us ladies out of there alive and unharmed. Quan slapped Marie because he didn't like how she was talking to him about what ZJ was doing to Kaia.

ZJ raped Kaia. He came out of the back, laughing evilly. You could tell he was up to no good. His shirt was off, one sock on, and he was trying to pull up his pants, which were halfway down with his zipper open. ZJ said how he was through with her anyway, and we could go ahead and leave because he got what he wanted. Nikita couldn't find her phone. She remembered she had put her phone in her pocketbook, which was in the trunk of the car. Kaia's phone was dead, and my battery was dying. Before we could get out of the house, the guys wanted to make sure we kept our mouths shut about what happened. So, they blocked the door so we couldn't leave.

Marie and I got guns pointed to our faces and Nikita got a knife drawn to her neck and Kaia had a broken beer bottle to her neck. All Marie could say to her boyfriend was, "Really? You gonna do me like that? Point yo gun to my face and do what? Shoot me?" She then realized he didn't love her, and it was time for her to leave him alone. Kaia blamed herself for what happened and felt like she signed up for this to happen.

If we had known what was going to take place that night, we would have never been there. Kaia feared that no one would believe us because we were under the influence of substances and alcohol. A lot of people remain quiet about rape and abuse because of the fear of people just assuming they consented to sex, that they would be judged from the drugs found in their system or just afraid what people will say about them. Neither of us girls ever got the authorities involved.

Marie is no longer with Quan. We found out ZJ, who had raped Kaia, ended up going to prison charged with felony charges for other things he had done. Karma caught up with him. The Lord will send help just in time. He's an on time God. Kaia is now going on 18 months clean because she received help from Alcoholics Anonymous. Nikita is still shooting up and Marie is still struggling with pills and weed. We don't hang out together anymore because we have all taken separate paths. We are still connected on social media and are able to see how each other is doing every now and then.

After all that He had brought me through, I knew it was time to appreciate and take my relationship with God seriously. He didn't allow me to be exposed to or contract any deadly sexual diseases or infections. I would schedule doctor visits to get checkups and STD tests because I didn't always use protection when I did have sex, and, by the grace of God, my results would come back negative. I am grateful that He covered me in my own stupidity.

My Heavenly Father delivered me from the destructive relationships I kept finding myself in, as I was dealing with men and women. My situationships with females were based on my own "free-flowing" sexual desires. The truth is, my "free-flowing" desires came from something that had me bound down since I was in the third grade. I got attacked by the spirit of perversion from a friend of the family, who was supposed to be like blood. I was at my older cousin's house to get my hair done. My cousin got a phone call and had to leave to handle some business. She told me to be good and do what I'm told while she's gone. I was "the business" she should have been attending, instead of leaving me with this lady. The friend of the family was a supposed trusted person.

After my cousin left, the woman kept commenting and saying that I was a pretty little girl and how she liked how my cousin fixed my hair all pretty. She said we were going to play a game called "House," where I would get to play as a grown up. After my cousin left, the woman kept commenting and saying that I was a pretty little girl and how she liked how my cousin fixed my hair all pretty. She said we were going to play a game called "House," where I would get to play as a grown up. "You will be the mom, and I'll be the dad," she said. So, what started off as a harmless kid's game became a harmful reality for me."

She said, "Be a good wife and do what I say." "Husbands cook for their wives sometimes, so eat this sandwich and chips, and you'll get some purple bag skittles when the game is over." Then she said, "Wives kiss their husbands on the lips as a thank you for doing nice things for them." She rubbed on my body inappropriately to get me to relax, so that I wouldn't be so tense and stiff for what she was getting ready to do to me. She started to kiss me on my neck and forcefully bent me over and started to dry hump me while I leaned against the living room couch.

All I could do was look out the window from the curtains, which were slightly see through, hoping that my cousin would pull up any minute. Her actions were followed by her unbuttoning my pants and fingering my private area. My stomach was upset, and I was nauseous after what had taken place. I was in the bathroom throwing up by the time my older cousin came back, and I was told by the lady to say it's nothing wrong with me, that I had gotten sick from eating too much candy.

That experience opened the doorway to identity confusion for me because I started to be more interested in girls and was not sure who I was. My hurt caused me to develop different versions of myself that didn't align with the Word of God. I took on identities that I was never called to carry. God calls us to maturity, and the enemy wants us to be called out of the character of Christ. I had to pray for God to bring me into oneness with Him, so that I wouldn't be divided within myself. I had to pray against the transferring spirits that were placed on me when people hurt me.

Someone hurt the lady who touched and misused me in a perverted way, so she transferred her hurt onto me, even though I was an innocent child. Instead of giving our hurts to God, we carry them around bleeding and transferring our pains to other people. How could I end up liking something that was done wrongly to me? As I got older, I struggled behind closed doors, battling with my sexuality. My freedom to explore with women was based on a twisted nightmare of what took place when I never received the help that I needed to cope with what had happened to me, which left me with ungodly sexual desires for women and men.

As far as men, I didn't have the best examples of what love was or how a man should treat a woman. I grew up finding myself in situationships with manipulative, controlling, verbally, mentally, and physically abusive men. As a young girl growing up, I said I would never allow a man to treat me the way I saw my dad handle women. Then as I grew older, I started walking in that curse, settling for men that didn't deserve me. That caused my aggression towards men, and I was so defensive, ready to fight back.

I remember one evening when my dad, one of my sisters, his girlfriend and I were coming from Hallsboro, NC. My dad and his girlfriend were fighting while us two kids were in the back. His girlfriend took the toy guitar I had and hit him in the head while he was driving with his left hand and hitting her with his right hand. Thank God we didn't wreck. He beat her so badly. I was exposed at a young age to violence, drugs, sex, and fast money. I had behaviors that were a reflection of what I grew up around and learned in my past.

A lot of people know me as a sweetheart and a good girl, but there were others who experienced my walk on the wild side. I mishandled myself and allowed others to mishandle me. I had this perfect wall built up, like I "had it all together," but the truth is, I was becoming someone who just wanted to numb the pain and not actually take the steps to heal, so the pain would go away. People would always tell me I'm different, and it's something about me that shines and sticks out. I can say at 24 years old that I am finally seeing the true me. I was uniquely created, and God blessed me with an energetic and vibrant personality.

Some people may not want to face reality, but there will come a time in our lives where we will have to face it so that we can experience true freedom. The truth is, life happens, and when it happens, we tend to hide our feelings and emotions to keep ourselves from being hurt even more. Questions linger in our minds like, "If I open up and be vulnerable, what does that lead me to?"

It is best to face your reality through the Word of God. God will bring your understanding of the Word through His Holy Spirit. I felt I wasn't good enough, which led me into deeper feelings of unworthiness and that I was too dirty for God to want anything to do with me. The best way to end a lie is with the truth. "PUT THAT WORD ON THE DEVIL," as my spiritual mentor Ozella would say.

I am learning more about myself daily, and I'm able to accept more of who I am becoming in Christ. God is teaching me to be confident in who He has called me to be. I am proud to say it has been 17 months since I had sex with anyone, and I have brought myself two purity rings and gifted myself with my second abstinence ring this past year. I did have a few slip ups with masturbation because I was dealing with sexual frustration.

Even now, I have to pray and ask the Lord to sustain me until it's time for my special someone to come into my life. I thank the Lord that my body is working properly. I still face temptation from guys trying to get with me, but I'm focused and know what I want. I have given myself fully to God.

"He is my Husbandman," as my spiritual mentor Darlene would say.

It has been a year since I had any type of drugs in my system, and I rarely drink. I have learned to be proud of myself and walk boldly with my head held high. I now dance for God and use my body for His glory, doing lyrical praise dance and dramatic mime ministry. God blessed me to have peace, so He could use me for His glory.

1st John 1:9 states, *"If we confess our sins, He is faithful and just to forgive us our sins, and to cleanse us from all unrighteousness."* Now I am able to come out about all God blessed me to overcome and share my experiences with others to let them know they don't have to hide in the dark alone and unashamed. Chances are in God's hands. If others don't want to forgive you for your past and the mistakes you made, know that Jesus offers you a life of forgiveness, love, joy, acceptance, healing, wholeness, and sanctification. You get a fresh start with God, new chances never fail with him; but time does run out, because we never know when it will be time for us to get called Home.

I learned to not take back any of my mistakes. From every sin God delivered me from, I can now use my life to help bring other young women and young people out of bondage and let them know there is a man that loves us unconditionally. That He offers a life more pleasing than this world could ever give. That you can be open with God and not have to sell yourself short. I challenge you today to choose to move forward. You can release your past because you no longer live there.

I want you to know that YOU ARE AMAZING. I believe in you. I can relate to what it's like to have emotional pain and have toxic ways of dealing with that pain. No matter how many times you fall, I'm cheering for you to pick yourself up and try again. We all have a part to play in this world. I want you to know that you are needed somewhere. You are the answer to someone's prayer. It's not too late to reach the full potential that you desire. God accepts YOU and loves you UNCONDITIONALLY.

Ask God to slow your role, so you can be in alignment with Him.

Here is one of my poems I wrote while in the transition of learning how to live in freedom and move forward:

Lost and Found

Looking around, it's nowhere to hide
Who can I run to with this divided mind
Sunken in by time
Remembering the wounds
That took place in the darkened rooms
The shame that is undeniably untamed
Who am I? What is my name?
Not the name given here by my parents on Earth
: But Great I Am who formed
You and I from the dirt

Am I really lost or just being hidden?
From the enemies who are in the shadows waiting
for my good riddance
Wishing for me to die, causing much turmoil,
bringing many tears to my eyes
But as I sit with this pen and paper
Using this writing as a form of a prayer
To my Creator
My heart is screaming, How much longer, Lord?

I'm feeling tied up in bondage,
free me from these demonic spiritual cords
As my present body, lay deep in the past
Knowing the old things are behind me but my
mind makes the memories last

But when I go to the Friend who sticks closer than
a Brother
He provides an unfailing love like no other
Jesus reminds me that I am no longer lost
I've already been found
He is the One who pulls me up out of the slimy pit
and places my feet on solid ground.

Chapter Nine

Fix Your Thoughts

God is working things out behind the scenes. Unexpected doors are opening for you. There is a door God opened for me that came with more than what I prayed for. I encourage you to keep praying and trusting, through whatever you are going through. He will deliver. Even in your storm, God is lining up the sunshine to come forth after the rain. Doors are getting ready to be opened for you that add to your life and not take away from your growth.

God allowed the enemy to pursue me but didn't give him permission to take me out. I realized that God used this experience to draw me closer so that He could accomplish what was set out to be fulfilled in my life. Here are a few questions to think about when it comes to fixing your thoughts so that you can maintain a spirit of joy.

1. Where do you find your thoughts traveling to?

2. Do your thoughts make you feel like you need a vacation from your own mind?

3. What thoughts do you allow to run rapidly?

4. What stops you from taking authority over those thoughts that plague your mind?

5. What do you believe about yourself?

My thoughts were impulsive and caused me to be insensitive towards myself. I often took my thoughts and convinced myself that those were God's thoughts towards me. I projected how I was feeling about myself and based how God felt about me on that. Of course, I was wrong, based on Isaiah 53:8-9.

See this paragraph from a spiritual sense. The lies in my mind were starving the truth from my heart. The eyes and ears of my heart would speak out to me about the pain I was feeling. I was crying from within. Your sight is what you currently see, and your vision is what you see for yourself that lies ahead. Your thoughts affect your sight and vision. Learning to view life with God's vision, being a visionary, means having to learn how to break down the vision and set realistic expectations. When you feel like you have not met the expectations you set for yourself, look at how much you have progressed and meditate on that with a thankful heart.

God's spirit is with you everywhere you go.

I had to become who I was looking for. I looked to people to bring me security. I had to learn how to stand on my own. Part of learning how to stand on your own is learning how to think for yourself. Now that I'm by myself, I don't have anyone giving me ungodly advice or making decisions for me. God has blessed me with the wisdom to think right and be positive. God had to teach me how to take my boxing gloves off. I was walking in mistrust towards everyone. I had to learn how to form relationships that come with freedom.

I had to learn how to take my time and slow down. I would have people at an arm's length distance because of my inability to really let people in to help me. God blessed me to get the right support. My spiritual support comes from my awesome church family at Shabach Nation of Praise with Bishop C.C. Dixon, a mighty man of God. Being in a church community with believers filled with the Holy Spirit and with a Bishop who carries the real anointing of God. I'm blessed for God to have aligned me with a sharpshooter in the Spirit like C.C. Dixon.

I also receive professional cognitive behavioral therapy at a facility that offers both mental health and addiction treatment. I am also receiving medication therapy for my traumatic anxiety and depression. At first, I was against medicine because of the experience I had with drugs, but I am able to handle prescribed medicine correctly without misusing it. Your traumatic experiences don't have to end you, but you can end them from hindering you and stopping you from having a prosperous new beginning.

Psalm 31:24 KJV tells us, *"To be of good courage and he shall strengthen your heart, all ye that hope in the Lord."* I often found myself battling against the inner critic within me. Do I believe that I can really do this? My prayer was, "God help my unbelief." I had to decide if I was going to commit to quitting or commit to progressing. I chose progression. I grew tired of making excuses for myself and coming into agreement with thoughts of defeat. The old Tiaina's time was up. It was time to stop fearing success and self-betterment. I could not continue to sabotage my growth.

When you are feeling scared of falling back into the same patterns as temptations rise, visualize yourself being lifted by His mighty Holy Hand. It will keep you from falling short because when you are in His presence, you can do no harm because all your focus is on him. Shifting your mind to see out of your vision versus your sight is how you can get through. Until the storm calms down, hold tight to your vision. If you are in God's presence, you don't have to take matters into your own hands. You just need to lift your hands and praise Him. The stronger the attack, the higher God is lifting you.

Connection is required to trust someone. Trust is personal. You have to be familiar with a person that you can trust, you have to know them. A lot of people find it hard to trust in things that they can't see, but God speaks and shows himself present every day in creation, in His Word, and even in your life. Invite God in, pray to Him and say, "Heavenly Father, I want to experience you on a more personal level. God help me to accept and prepare for how You show up. Help me not to fight how you choose to show me how personal you are but help me to embrace you no matter the circumstances." God knows that we need time to learn how to trust in Him. Sometimes we need to over-come a challenge to strengthen our spirits. Trust comes as we go through hardships and experience God as our deliverer.

God cares about your broken heart.

One of the ways I practiced meditating and fix-ing my thoughts was by going on nature prayer walks. There was a trail that connected to a lake near my apartment. One day, while I was on a na-ture prayer walk with God, He allowed me to see the most beautiful thing. It was this lady with her dog. It looked like the dog had gotten into an acci-dent. It only had three legs, but he was still push-ing forth. He had his tongue sticking out, enjoying the breeze. His tail was wagging, and he wasn't afraid to keep going.

As I observed them, I noticed that the owner was running with their dog. At first, I thought she was going too fast for the dog. As I looked closer, the dog was enjoying the run. God showed me that we don't have to allow our limitations to limit us. We all just need the right someone to push us, to help us keep going, and He will put someone in our lives to do just that.

That analogy made me think about the good

graces of the Lord. No matter how many people may leave us when we are not deemed normal, but He is still here, pushing us to go forth. Life happens, and we have unexpected problems that come up, and it causes our normal lives to be interrupted. God teaches us that with Him we can go on. Losing a leg wouldn't be able to stop God's goodness and mercy from reaching us. Nothing that we go through in life can keep us separated from the love of God.

We may go through accidents, we may lose people, and other life changing events, but the beautiful thing is that God never changes. We can trust Him and stand on his solid rock. No matter how bruised we may get from what happens to us, God is ready to lift us up in his hands and give us greater strength and joy like never before. We may not understand why certain things happen to us but when we acknowledge that God's love is flowing through us, we don't become bitter.

Accidents can cause use to lose the ability to walk, talk, see, or hear, and at first, we may have a hard time dealing with these life changing circumstances. We may experience sadness, hopelessness and just become cast down with darkness, but once we invite God in, He replaces all that with joy. He clothes us in His truth, that we still have life left in us. We may have suffered some losses, but we are still standing and still breathing. It shows we still have a purpose.

Some of us have been through experiences that were supposed to kill us, and God's grace covered us through it all. Each time we wake up, it is God's way of showing us that He loves us. He whispers to us sweetly, "I got you. I will carry you. I will love you, and I will give you peace that surpasses your understanding." God is so real. He is a promise keeper. As I look back over my life, I've been through things that were supposed to make me lose my mind. If God can keep me, then I'm here to tell you that God can keep you as well. God has not forgotten you. As you continue to read on, I want you to know that things are working for your good. Down the line, you will see how God will get the glory from your life. God can use your life for His purpose even when you feel unusable.

We serve a supernatural God, who makes ways out of no ways. I don't know what your situation is, but I want you to know that God gives you gifts daily. Each day is a gift, it's something we have never seen before. When you allow God to be your strength, you can still make something great out of your day. No matter what your day-to-day routine is, you have the opportunity to make a difference in your life.

There is nothing so big that we go through that our God can't see us through. No matter how big the giants in your life may look, God is the ultimate giant slayer. Your hard seasons don't last always. Your challenging seasons build character in you. You may be in the beginning of a rough patch in your life, and you don't see how you can go on. You have to seize and take authority over your life. Don't allow your circumstances to overtake you. Speak to your situation and tell it, "My God is seeing me through." Remind your circumstances that God specializes in the impossible.

Joy comes in the morning. Each of our mornings may look different. Morning could represent a day, weeks, or months of weeping and crying out to God. Just when you think all hope is lost, our Heavenly Father comes in the morning and things start to turn around for you. You are able to go on with life. You start to see the light shine through the cracks of your pain. Keep praying, even if you have to pray all night. Your prayer is what will refresh you and what will renew you. When we are able to take our eyes off of ourselves and shift our focus on Jesus and what he has done here on Earth, it shifts things.

As we look at the power of the Holy Spirit, how Jesus rose from the dead and overcame death, it speaks to us to let us know we will overcome. Circumstances might make us feel as if we are dying, but when we shift our minds, our spirits will start to rise. We will feel ourselves starting to rise out of the darkness. Depression, sadness, sickness, bitterness, and anger starts to flee from us because we know we serve a resurrected King, who will resurrect us. We have to believe that Jesus has brought us too far to leave us in the pit of hopelessness.

When you pray to God, it gives you a new vision. As you pray to Him to take the scales off your eyes, it will help you see His goodness that is in front of you. The new day that you are walking in doesn't have to be like yesterday. I understand you may be facing the same problems as yesterday, but today is a new day for you to shift your mindset and look at your problems differently.

It's not for us to understand how God will make the way. We have to allow our hearts to be our eyes. What we see with our eyes will only weigh us down. When we allow our hearts to be our eyes, we are able to walk with our heads held high. We know in our hearts that God is a God of justice. We forget that God plays multiple roles in our lives. Challenge yourself to learn the names of God and pray to Him according to the names you need Him to show up as. Our heart reminds us that He is a healer, deliverer, provider, our hope, a friend, miracle worker, promise keeper, and infinite meaning His ways are not like our ways, our comforter, and so much more.

You may feel abandoned and alone. Though God is unseen, He is presently there working and fighting on your behalf. I pray that whenever you feel alone, your heart is constantly reminded that He has His heavenly angels guarding and protecting you. May you get a new belief in your heart that his heavenly angels are clearing your path for you, that God is making things happen for you right now in this hour.

Chapter Ten

Inner Healing

Healing is ready to meet each of us with open arms of wholeness. We can convince ourselves that healing emotionally hurts so much that we should avoid it, so we just continue on in broken patterns. We would rather remain hurt than pull the bandages off our wounds that resulted from being cut deep in our heart, stabbed in the back and life's disappointments. The offset of our emotions sometimes seems unmanageable, especially for women. Men tend to mask their emotions and suffer silently, which is why suicide rates are increasing rapidly. When we believe it's better to suffer silently, mentally and emotionally, the infection of pain only gets worse and births a bigger out of denial that healing is needed. It's easy to remain hurt because you may believe you will never get better.

The journey to wholeness begins once we stop suppressing what we feel within. We have to address this in order to get to a specific location, right? It is the same with the process of healing. How can we know where we are going in life if we don't address what's within? Your inner destination determines your outer location. If you feel lost and hopeless on the inside, you will find yourself in places that are lost and hopeless. On the shoulders of trouble are endurance (Romans 5:3) or idleness.

Imagine we have an angel and a devil on each shoulder. When we are in trouble, we have two choices to make. We can lean to the angel's side, which helps us to endure and persevere to live a hopeful, faith-filled life. On the devil's side, there is more trouble. The devil tries to build an idle mind, which is the devil's playground where he roams and marks territory within your whole being. When trouble appears to take hold of you, it can have a tight grip if you let it.

Without a point of direction, we will continue to circle around the block in our minds, denying how empty we feel and deny the fear of being vulnerable with anyone. In doing this, we deny ourselves the actual care we need. When I realized that God knows the worst and best about me, all the good and bad decisions I have ever made, it gave me hope of being restored and made new from the inside out.

I often found myself in guilt cycles, which only made me feel worse as I allowed self-destructive behaviors to grow within me. I lost all sense of self-control, and I wanted to ease the pain I was feeling my way. The way of the world, which separated me even further from God. I was so dependent on man. I just wanted to be loved and I did not want to be alone. I wanted to always have someone around as a distraction, just so I wouldn't have to just sit with Tiaina.

I grew into an adult, but I still carried the broken child who was hurt, disappointed, desperate for acceptance, had low self-esteem, identity confusion, was rejected, and was lonely. The little me was starting to become too heavy for the big me, and I knew it was time to release her. The adult me cried for help when all I could see in the mirror was a child who felt abandoned and trapped in an adult body.

My mind and heart were filled with addictions of the flesh, while my mouth was praising God. I was confessing with my mouth, "Lord, bless me to know You better," but my heart wanted to know how I could continue to please my flesh. I had to pray and ask the Lord to deliver me from myself. My prayer went something like this: "I know you care for me; God help me to care for myself so that I don't give up and continue to make choices that will allow me to throw my life down the drain."

A lot of people offer God lip service, but their hearts are only serving themselves. Then we sit and have the nerve to point someone else's sin out, except for what we are doing behind closed doors. Hiding the parts of our lives we don't want others to see or know about. Titus 1:16 CSB reads, *"They claim to know God, but they deny him by their works. They are detestable, disobedient and unfit for any good work."* The truth is that God's mercy needs to continuously reach us all so that we will be transformed by His holy Word and Holy Spirit.

When you have been down for so long, you learn there is much significance in the rise.

Our habits are based upon our self-control or lack thereof. What we do repeatedly comes from a devotion to a specific thing. What we do either controls us or we end up controlling it. The world tells us to "do you," help yourself by doing what makes you "happy," but what about when what brings you "fulfillment" brings you harm? When I started to find myself in ungodly environments do-ing only God knows what, I knew I needed help.

Someone may be reading this book and feel like they have serious demons they are battling with. What you are battling may scare others away, but with God, it draws Him closer to us because He understands we are in pain and in need of some-one to bring us out of it. Our God is a Holy God, and when we come to Him our once stained lives are washed away and made free. He's not afraid of our sin.

As you take one step towards getting the help you need, God will take the necessary steps to bless you. When you put pride aside, promotion comes in. It is in our obedience that blessings follow. Like the sunshine that comes after the storm and rain, there is a rebirth that takes place in inner healing. As you work towards releasing the old, it brings in the new. A birthing pain that comes with the new. A lot of us are spiritually carrying overgrown ba-bies that are ready to be birthed. This goes for men too, see it in a spiritual sense. God has a purpose for all of us.

We have to be intentional about our intimacy with God. When we are intimate with God there is a spiritual conception that produces physical birth. We can't give birth to what God places on the inside of us without spending time with him. In the midst of contractions, there is an ease that comes with giving birth. When you stick to God's plan and follow His direction, you are able to be birthed to another level in Him.

There is a sound that produces a move of God. Our stories, our pain, who we are, is all in our voice. The voice is powerful. It's the sound from deep within. When you have been down for so long, you learn there is much significance in the rise. You have seen the worst of the worst, and you don't fear loss or defeat. There is strength in seeing the darkness you are up against, to know that you feel weak, but you were chosen for the fight. In your fallen stage, you learn from the mistakes you made. As you rise, it teaches you who to avoid and what to avoid. Your mistakes represent tiny pebbles. Those pebbles form into big rocks the more mistakes you make. The rocks cause you to sink, but God steps in and causes you to rise. He builds a new foundation in you.

You gain experience and wisdom from what you went through, and you learn to apply it to future situations. There is something about having nothing that produces something in you. When you're at the bottom, you see things for what they really are. When you are on top, sometimes you can be blinded by your own "success." We have to experience being in a low place in life to make sure we never go there again. It's a way of refreshing us, to help us realize we only need God and that we can't be high and mighty on our own.

Being at the bottom teaches you lessons you would never have been able to learn at the top. Being broken down causes vulnerability. When you're vulnerable, you become open to being taught. When we are on top, we think we know it all and have it all. In reality, with this perspective, we only labor in vain because our foundation was built on faulty human ground, filled with pride, ego, and selfishness. We need God for everything. No matter how powerful you are in your human abilities, you have someone higher than you that you have to answer to. You have to be stripped from everything that makes you feel mighty to build true character. Nothing happens that God doesn't give a "Yes" to.

When you come from the bottom, you can overcome anything. To really shine in the light, you have to know what it feels like to be in the darkness. The bottom gives your divine strategy when you connect with God. You get time to reflect, plan, and accomplish your way back up with God leading you. We have to be broken down to see that God is not done with us yet. God takes us from level to level. It's easy to feel accomplished and think there is no room to grow. There is always inner work that needs to be done in us.

When God comes in like a mighty wind, you not only feel Him but hear Him through His movement. Zechariah 10:8 NIV says, *"I will whistle for them to gather them together, For I have redeemed them, and they will be as numerous as they were before."* When the Lord whistles and calls forth everything pertaining to you, near and far, to come. What is for you will show up without delay. What once was a hindrance for you in the past will be no more. God's favor will cause you to move quickly toward what God has in store for you.

My inner work began as God showed me myself. I needed to be free from unforgiveness, hate and the bondage of pleasing people, and always saying yes to things I didn't want to do. Many people live in bondage to pleasing people, but they don't see it as an unhealthy thing. In reality, I had become a puppet, doing what other people said and demanded.

I lost who I was when I continued to be in tune with what others thought about me. My identity became wrapped around what people would say, and I didn't realize at the time that I didn't have to answer to what was being said. I was ignoring my own heart just to tend to someone else's. I started to hate people for how I allowed them to treat me when I had the power to stop it.

I learned that it's about taking accountability, recognizing where these problems are stemming from, and taking the steps to heal properly. How can we properly enjoy and endure the fullness of God and experience being free if we don't work on removing what's holding us down? It's all about paradise right here, in the land of the living. We have to learn to not let our trials and circumstances make us feel like we are living the life of the dead. We can be alive but yet feel so lifeless, numb, hopeless, angry, and resentful. I once felt all these emotions.

Keep in mind, of course, that you have to be consistent. Without consistency, you will find yourself going back to old habits and behaviors that are not healthy. Your fruitful season is right around the corner. It's more than just religion. It's about that spiritual connection that God gives us with His truth, and once you experience Him personally and understand the love He has for you, you will see that it is a love out of this world.

A lot of people walk around with heavy hearts and masks on their faces, with so much childhood trauma and hurt built up on the inside. Some people think that is just who they are. I was one of them. I never thought that I could get to this healthy part of myself. I have a long way to go, but I can tell you that when you become one with God and yourself, it changes your view. If we are all wounded, will the dysfunctional living ever stop?

It's not about the uncontrollable things that happen to us, but what we choose to do with them. I had serious unresolved childhood trauma, abandonment issues, attachment issues, and rejection trauma. If you're reading this and can relate, I want you to know that no matter how long you have been hurting deep down, you can be free from the bondage you're in. Don't beat yourself down about the past. We have to heal and let go of that heavy stuff we carry around in our heart so that we can walk into the fullness of healing and greatness. When you have a clear mind and heart, you feel like you are capable of doing anything with God on your side.

Many people live with regret because they spend their whole life and so much time trying to please a loved one, whether that's family or friends, while sacrificing their own ability to live. If you are driven to only do and be what the person expects of you, then, in a way, you have lost the ability to live. It takes us being hurt deeply to realize something has to change within ourselves. I have learned to have control over me, and if someone can't respect me, they don't deserve to be around me. Family or not, this goes for anyone. I thank God for the heartbreaks and disappointments because everything I have been through played a part in shaping me for the better. I pray the same for you as well.

Chapter Eleven

Called to Love

As you embrace this closing chapter, I pray that your heart and mind will be open to an acceptable God-given right called "love," to grasp on to true love and not the familiarity we call "love" disguised as lust. We are called to love the Lord our God with all our heart, soul, mind, and strength. Then we are called to love our neighbor as ourselves. What about loving those who do you wrong? How can you love when you feel like you have nothing left of you to give? When you believe in something, you feel it in your heart. You can't believe in what you don't feel. You have to experience the realness of God's love to know how to love.

When you feel the love of God, then you can believe in truly loving others. Whenever you allow Scripture to be your guide, the word trains you to love one another. We find out how to love and live in Scripture. David asked in the 51st Psalm for God to create in him a clean heart and a renewed spirit. We don't have to be afraid to ask God to help. He will answer that prayer graciously and quickly. He longs for us to walk beside Him.

Even through your sorrows, know that God still holds your tomorrow.

Some may read this chapter and say, "I can't forgive this person because they raped me, abused me, took advantage of me," or whatever it is that person did to hurt you. I'm a witness that it is possible to forgive those who have done the worst to you. God will not have His people ignorant of Satan's devices (read 2 Corinthians 2:11). I had to be quiet as the Lord instructed me that He would handle it all. Just trust Him. So, I had to learn to forgive and love while also being kind to the people who were causing and sending me harm.

The devil was working through family and people I thought were friends to attempt to destroy me. Talk about pain and feeling like you are unable to forgive. At one point, I thought my suffering was unbearable. See, my Heavenly Father was taking on everything being thrown at me. During those times of affliction, God poured his Spirit into me to protect, shield, and empower me like never before. I had to show love, kindness, and forgiveness to enemies. I couldn't take matters into my own hands.

I was once an enemy of God because of my sinful ways, and he forgave me. That's what makes it easier to forgive others and leave the rest in God's hand. Before the Lord allowed me to see in the Spiritual Realm what was taking place behind my back, I would be able to feel the hate radiate out of the person's body. I would feel fine, but every time I went around these particular people, I would feel sick and not know why. God was showing me all along how people felt about me, but I was so naive and blinded because I was trying to see the good in everyone. I was wrapped up in webs of deception. My kindness for weakness, and I was being suffocated by people.

> *"Do not repay evil with evil or insult to with insult. On the contrary, repay evil with blessing, because to this you were called so that you may inherit a blessing." — Peter 3:9 NIV*

For every time I cried, God had me in a place where he restored me with double laughter and joy. Even in the midst of attacks, God kept me in a safe resting place. He gave me a double portion of what my mom didn't carry out because of the physical sickness she faced. The mantle doesn't go back to Heaven. God builds you for what He calls you to carry. Every affliction I had to go through doubled God's glory in my life.

He blessed me with the ability to write and use my pain as a guide for my purpose. My pain led me to get understanding from God. I learned to never forget him. When I felt like the storms and rain had overtaken me, God saved me. The storms and rain of life taught me how to hope in God's Word. Though I had many people against me and even brought trouble to myself because of my sinful way of living, God blessed me to tell this part of my story to help bless others. I hope that my story has brought you motivation and encouragement. We want things to come easy, but we have to go through trials and learn to trust that God will work it out.

God does not save and deliver us from our old ways and habits so that we can turn our backs on people who are struggling with the same things we once struggled with. God's love is more than just for our own personal benefit; it is for everyone. He died for the whole world, so His love is for everyone. We cannot become so consumed with self-righteousness that we become judgmental as if we never did anything wrong.

Judgment on others only creates an environment that's restricted, therefore making it impossible for people to go to anyone in their time of weakness. If someone is already bound to the sin that easily ensnares them, why should judgment of man be added to the shackles of guilt of the person who's already feeling imprisoned from the inside out. Titus 3:3–7 NIV states: *"At one time we too were foolish, disobedient, deceived and enslaved by all kinds of passions and pleasures. We lived in malice and envy, being hated and hating one another. But when the kindness and love of God our Savior appeared he saved us, not because of righteous things we had done, but because of his mercy. He saved us through the washing of Rebirth and Renewal by the Holy Spirit whom he poured out on us generously through Jesus Christ our Savior, so that, having the hope of eternal life."*

I wrote this chapter as I was sitting in my car. It had been a pretty rainy day so far. While I was writing, the mailman drove by. As the truck passed by, it made me think how we still have a job to do even in "undeliverable" circumstances. No one likes to drive the storm or rain. We enjoy sunshine and beautiful blue skies. The mailman teaches us that we still have people connected to us with packages that need to be delivered. If I had allowed defeat and uncertainty to kick in, I wouldn't have been able to deliver with this book.

As a mail carrier, you may be given packages and have to go places you have never been before, walking in territories of the unknown, not knowing if there is a mean dog waiting to chase you or a friendly smile waiting to greet you at the door. As you work your way around the neighborhood, you take notes and become comfortable because you learn what works and what doesn't work. We don't wait for the mailman to come on a pretty day; we want our packages and mail to come when it's due, not when it's a good time to receive them. When the fire and high waters come, will you still get out and deliver what the world needs?

Our worst times show us that dreams still come true. You have to believe in yourself. To believe in yourself, is to believe in God, who created you for greater works. We are all mail carriers. We are not meant to keep what's assigned to us to ourselves, even when it's raining, snowing, or whatever circumstance is present. As a carrier of God's glory, you still have to release, work, and go forth, no matter the time of day or circumstance.

So many people are suffering from mental illness and suicidal tendencies. Whether we want to admit it or not, we all need at least one person in our corner to uplift and encourage us. I have so many other parts of my life and experiences I want to share, but that's for other books. I know I won't be able to reach everyone, but for you reading this book, I challenge you to go forth and tell your story boldly and unashamedly so that you can help others who are silently suffering and hiding in the dark. I used to feel stuck in my circumstances because the storms in my life were filled with heavy rain. I couldn't see anything greater coming. Everyone may not support or receive you but know there will be people out there who would understand your language. Will you deliver?

God uses what He has already provided for you to bring about the miracle you need. Sometimes, we can doubt and say, "Is that God telling me to do that?" Do it anyway. He honors your obedience just because you thought you were doing what honors Him. The instruction that seems so small to you is what leads you to see the biggest breakthrough over your life.

God blessed me with someone who under-stands me personally, who has been through simi-lar experiences, and has passed on much wisdom to me. My spiritual mentor Yolanda, who I also jokingly call my Fairy Godmother, would always make me laugh and say "FGM In da house." Yolanda is married with two beautiful daughters. She took time out of her busy schedule to genuine-ly pour into me whenever I needed her. She is the definition of the importance of never being too busy for people you intentionally want to make time for. Yolanda was able to reach me with the Word of God right on time. She took the time to remind me that I don't have to perform for God, and that He doesn't love me based on my accom-plishments.

Have faith that God will do greater things through your life.

She prayed with me through depression, temp-tations, addictions of the flesh, and even when I felt like I had no purpose for being here. When I felt discouraged, she didn't let me stay down in the dumps. She would tell me, "Girl, be excited! Get up and go on Facebook and find some people to en-courage. Pick up the phone and plant a word in somebody's heart." She always reminded me not to worry about the money I don't have or the next step I don't have, but to look at all I do have and use it for God.

What's within your reach that you can use to reach others and inspire those around you? My phone, pen, and paper were within my reach. I had to learn how to sit at God's feet, hear His voice, and let people know what thus says the Lord. I used what was within my reach to make encouraging videos for God's people. I started my YouTube channel, Comfort In Christ, one year ago.

I recently had to take a break to make sure I was putting God first, that I was sincerely after his heart and not just my spiritual gifts. I wanted to make sure my foundation was built on God and not myself. God had to align me with healing and wholeness, so I could come back better and stronger. I needed God to work on me behind the scenes. I prayed that God would make me more sensitive and aware of others' needs in the spiritual realm. I pray to be so aligned with God that I will be accurate in delivering the His people, and that I will be humble to allow Him to lead me. I asked God to give me His eyes to see, his ears to hear, and his heart to feel the brokenness in the world around me. Now that my first official published book is out, I am able to start doing my videos again and work towards my God vision.

Prayer for Called to Love

"I pray that out of his glorious, unlimited resources he will empower you with inner strength through his Spirit. Then Christ will make his home in your hearts as you trust in Him. Your roots will grow down into God's love and keep you strong. And may you have the power to understand, as all God's people should, how wide, how long, how high, and how deep his love is. May you experience the love of Christ, though it is too great to fully understand. Then you will be made complete with all the fullness of life and power that comes from God. Now all glory to God, who is able, through his mighty power at work within us, to accomplish infinitely more than we might ask or think. Glory to Him in the church and in Christ Jesus through all generations forever and ever! Amen." — Ephesians 3:16-21 NIV

About The Author

My name is Tiaina Doughty. I am a graduate from Fayetteville State University, with a major in Psychology and a minor in Criminal Justice. I am willing to learn for the betterment of myself. I enjoy being free and happy. Those who know me know I have a smile who can brighten up anyone's day, I love laughter, I can be goofy, and I like to have a good time. I like to show myself as friendly, willing to help others when I can. I have a heart for others where I find joy encouraging and being a prayer warrior for others. I love the Lord and I can minister to others from my pain as a witness that God can restore, heal and set free. God is working in me and through me by using the good, the bad and even the ugly circumstances to make me more useful for later plans in His continuously unfolding story for my life.

www.ingramcontent.com/pod-product-compliance
Lightning Source LLC
Chambersburg PA
CBHW070721130626
46553CB00005B/2095